D0532309

PANCAKES, CRÊPES
BLINTZES & BLINIS

PANCAKES, CRÊPES BLINTZES & BLINIS

More than 20 deliciously simple recipes for delectable treats, from pancakes, wraps and fruit-filled crêpes to latkes and griddled scones, shown step-by-step in over 125 beautiful photographs

Susannah Blake

LORENZ BOOKS

This edition is published by Lorenz Books

Lorenz Books is an imprint of Anness Publishing Ltd, Hermes House, 88–89 Blackfriars Road, London SE1 8HA; tel. 020 7401 2077; fax 020 7633 9499
www.lorenzbooks.com; www.annesspublishing.com

If you like the images in this book and would like to investigate using them for publishing, promotions or advertising, please visit our website www.practicalpictures.com for more information.

© Anness Publishing Ltd 2004, 2006

UK agent: The Manning Partnership Ltd, 6 The Old Dairy, Melcombe Road, Bath BA2 3LR; tel. 01225 478444; fax 01225 478440; sales@manning-partnership.co.uk

UK distributor: Grantham Book Services Ltd, Isaac Newton Way, Alma Park Industrial Estate, Grantham, Lincs NG31 9SD; tel. 01476 541080; fax 01476 541061; orders@gbs.tbs-ltd.co.uk

North American agent/distributor: National Book Network, 4501 Forbes Boulevard, Suite 200, Lanham, MD 20706; tel. 301 459 3366; fax 301 429 5746; www.nbnbooks.com

Australian agent/distributor: Pan Macmillan Australia, Level 18, St Martins Tower, 31 Market St, Sydney, NSW 2000; tel. 1300 135 113; fax 1300 135 103; customer.service@macmillan.com.au

New Zealand agent/distributor: David Bateman Ltd, 30 Tarndale Grove, Off Bush Road, Albany, Auckland; tel. (09) 415 7664; fax (09) 415 8892

Publisher: Joanna Lorenz
Editorial Director: Judith Simons
Senior Editor: Susannah Blake
Editorial Reader: Lindsay Zamponi
Designer: Adelle Morris
Photographers: Martin Brigdale, Nicky Dowey, Amanda Heywood, William Lingwood, Craig Robertson, Garreth Sambidge

Recipes: Pepita Aris, Alex Barker, Ghillie Basan, Joanna Farrow, Brian Glover, Sallie Morris, Jennie Shapter, Marlena Spieler, Sunil Vijayakar
Production Controller: Pedro Nelson

Previously published as *Pancakes and Crêpes*

10 9 8 7 6 5 4 3 2 1

NOTES

• Bracketed terms are intended for American readers.
• For all recipes, quantities are given in both metric and imperial measures and, where appropriate, in standard cups and spoons. Follow one set, but not a mixture, because they are not interchangeable.
• Standard spoon and cup measures are level. 1 tsp = 5ml, 1 tbsp = 15ml, 1 cup = 250ml/8fl oz.
• Australian standard tablespoons are 20ml. Australian readers should use 3 tsp in place of 1 tbsp for measuring small quantities of gelatine, flour, salt, etc.
• American pints are 16fl oz/2 cups. American readers should use 20fl oz/2.5 cups in place of 1 pint when measuring liquids.
• Electric oven temperatures in this book are for conventional ovens. When using a fan oven, the temperature will probably need to be reduced by about 10–20ºC/20–40ºF. Since ovens vary, you should check with your manufacturer's instruction book for guidance.
• Medium (US large) eggs are used unless otherwise stated.

Front cover shows Chive Pancakes with Pickled Herring p30 & Cranberry Sorbet in Lace Pancakes p60

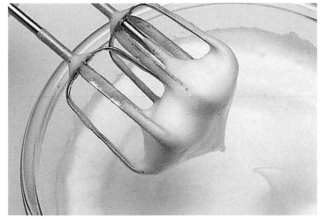

Contents

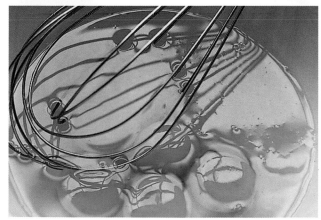

PANCAKES, CRÊPES, BLINTZES AND BLINIS

Pancakes are one of the oldest forms of bread and have been eaten since ancient times. Made from a simple batter poured on to a hot griddle or pan and cooked over a high heat, records of pancakes can be found dating back to Roman times. The tradition has survived through the centuries, and today virtually every country in the world has its own classic version.

France is the birthplace of the paper-thin crêpe, while thick potato *latkes* and sweet fruity *blintzes* come from the Jewish tradition. Bitesize *blinis* come from Russia, and simple drop scones from Scotland. In southern India, *dosas* made from a thick lentil batter are wrapped around spiced potatoes, while in China paper-thin *bao bing* are the classic accompaniment served with crispy Peking duck. In Thailand, sweet coconut *kanom kluk* are sold as street food, and in Japan traditional *dora yaki* are spread with sweet aduki bean paste and folded in half. Each one has its own unique blend of ingredients, individual preparation and cooking techniques.

Pancakes are a fantastically versatile food – perfect for the modern cook – and a multitude of different dishes can be made from the most basic of batters. Plain crêpes and pancakes are delicious eaten straight from the pan with a simple topping, but they are also fabulous filled with sweet or savoury ingredients, then served immediately, baked until piping hot, or fried in butter or oil until crisp and golden.

Thin batters can be swirled around the pan to produce paper-thin crêpes, or drizzled to make delicate, lacy pancakes. Thick batters can be spooned into the pan to produce simple, thick pancakes. Other ingredients such as shredded vegetables or chopped herbs can add substance to batters, while whisked egg whites, yeast, baking powder and fizzy liquids such as beer can all help to give batters a very light texture.

The variations are endless, and the results are always fantastic. Whether you're making a simple breakfast, a sophisticated appetizer, a hearty main meal or a sumptuous dessert, you will always find the perfect pancake.

Anti-clockwise from far left: pancakes are loved all over the world, and every country seems to have their own version: breakfast pancakes are an all-American classic; paper-thin crêpes come from France; buckwheat blinis from Russia; sweet blintzes from the Jewish tradition; and Mandarin pancakes from China.

MAKING BATTERS

The most basic pancake batter is made from flour, eggs and milk, whisked together until smooth, but there are many variations on this classic mixture. Batters may be thin or thick, depending on whether you need to swirl the batter to make thin crêpes or spoon it into the pan to make thicker griddle cakes.

The milk may be replaced or combined with other liquids such as water, wine or beer, and the batter may be sweetened with sugar, or flavoured with herbs, spices and aromatics. Grated vegetables such as potato or courgette (zucchini), or shredded leaves such as spinach or chard may be stirred into batters to give a thick, chunky result, or the mixture can be enriched with melted butter, yogurt, cream or cheese.

Different types of flour can be used, and each one gives a different result. Plain (all-purpose) flour is widely used for basic batters, while self-raising (self-rising) flour is often used to produce thick pancakes with a light texture. Wholemeal and buckwheat flours produce pancakes with a darker colour, more distinctive flavour and heavier texture. Other ingredients, such as ground lentils or matzo meal, can also be used to make batters, either combined with, or in place of, the flour.

Below: To make a basic batter, whisk the eggs together, then beat in the flour and milk.

BASIC CRÊPE BATTER

This simple egg, flour and milk batter is perfect for making plain crêpes, which can then be topped or filled with sweet or savoury mixtures. The batter should be the consistency of double (heavy) cream so that it can be swirled around the hot pancake pan leaving only the thinnest layer of batter. If the mixture is too thick, stir in a little more milk before cooking. For good results, it is important to leave the batter to stand for a short while before cooking. This recipe makes about 8 crêpes.

1 Break three eggs into a large bowl and beat well using an electric whisk. Start to beat in 115g/4oz/1 cup plain (all-purpose) flour until the mixture becomes too thick to continue. Beat a little milk into the mixture to loosen it slightly, then gradually beat in the remaining flour.

2 Very slowly, add 250ml/8fl oz/1 cup milk to the egg and flour paste, beating all the time until smooth. Cover the bowl with clear film (plastic wrap) and set aside to stand for about 20 minutes.

THICK PANCAKE BATTER

Small, thick pancakes are made with a slightly thicker batter that helps the pancakes to keep their shape during cooking. This slightly sweetened one is perfect for making Scottish drop scones. To make a savoury batter, omit the sugar and season with salt and freshly ground black pepper. This recipe makes about 18 pancakes.

1 Sift 225g/8oz/2 cups self-raising (self-rising) flour and 2.5ml/½ tsp salt into a bowl, then stir in 15ml/1 tbsp caster (superfine) sugar and make a well in the centre.

2 Pour 1 beaten egg and 150ml/¼ pint/⅔ cup milk into the well in the flour and gradually incorporate the flour to make a smooth paste. Beat in a further 150ml/ ¼ pint/⅔ cup milk to make a smooth batter.

FLAVOURING BASIC BATTERS

Plain pancake and crêpe batters can be transformed with the addition of basic flavourings and ingredients. Try some of the following.
• To give sweet batters a fresh, citrus flavour, stir in the zest of one lemon.
• To make a light savoury batter with a tangy flavour use beer in place of the milk; for sweet batters add sparkling or still wine.
• To add flavour and colour to plain batters, stir in about 30ml/2tbsp finely chopped herbs. Soft-leaved herbs such as tarragon and parsley are particularly good.
• To make deliciously cheesy pancakes, stir about 45ml/3tbsp freshly grated Parmesan cheese into a basic crêpe or savoury pancake batter.

LIGHTENING AND ENRICHING BASIC BATTERS

By altering the basic batter mix, you can affect the texture of the pancakes – making them lighter or richer, softer or chewier.
• To make a light, melt-in-the-mouth batter for thick pancakes, first separate the eggs. Make the batter using the yolks, then whisk the egg whites and fold these into the batter.
• To enrich pancake batters, use a mixture of half milk and half cream.
• To make a really rich, creamy batter, beat in 60ml/4 tbsp ricotta cheese.

Below: Flavour sweet batter with lemon zest, savoury batter with chopped herbs, or use beer instead of milk.

COOKING AND FLIPPING

Thin and thick batters are cooked in different ways. Crêpes are best cooked in a pan, but thick pancakes can be cooked either in a pan or on a griddle.

Right: Tossing crêpes can be great fun but often requires a bit of practice.

Below: Pour a thin layer of crêpe batter into the pan and, once cooked, stack the crêpe between sheets of kitchen paper.

COOKING CRÊPES
The secret to successful crêpes is to ensure the pan is hot enough before you add the batter. For the best results use a crêpe pan with a flat bottom and sides that angle straight out.

1 Heat a 20cm/8in crêpe pan over a medium heat until a few drops of water dropped on to the surface of the pan sizzle immediately. Grease the pan very lightly using butter or sunflower oil and ladle 45–60ml/3–4 tbsp batter into the pan. Quickly tilt and rotate the pan so that the batter spreads out to cover the base of it thinly and evenly, then pour out any excess batter.

2 Cook the crêpe for about 30 seconds, or until it is set and small holes start to appear in the surface. Carefully lift the edge of the crêpe using a palette knife (metal spatula); the underside should be lightly browned. Shake the pan back and forth vigorously to loosen the crêpe completely, then flip it over. (Toss it if you're feeling brave, or simply flip it over using the palette knife.)

3 Cook the crêpe for a further 30 seconds until golden underneath, then slide it on to a sheet of kitchen paper. Cook the remaining batter in the same way, stacking the crêpes between sheets of kitchen paper until ready to serve.

COOKING LACE PANCAKES

These pretty pancakes are made with crêpe batter and make a perfect dessert pancake, filled with ice cream, sorbet or fruit salad and dusted with icing (confectioners') sugar.

1 Heat a crêpe pan or small frying pan until a few drops of water dropped on to the surface of the pan sizzle immediately. Remove the pan from the heat.

2 Using a tablespoon, drizzle thin lines of batter over the bottom of the hot pan to produce a lace pattern. (The pancake should be about 14cm/5½in in diameter.) Return the pan to the heat for about 30 seconds. Using a palette knife (metal spatula), carefully lift up the edge of the pancake; it should be golden underneath.

3 Carefully turn the pancake over and cook for about 30 seconds, or until golden underneath. Slide the pancake on to a sheet of kitchen paper and cook the remaining batter in the same way, stacking the pancakes between sheets of kitchen paper.

COOKING THICK PANCAKES

Thick pancakes such as drop scones can be cooked on a hot griddle or in a frying pan or pancake pan.

1 Lightly oil a griddle or pan and heat until hot. Drop in tablespoons of batter to make three or four small pancakes, and cook for about 30 seconds, or until bubbles start to appear on the surface. Carefully lift up the edge of the pancakes using a palette knife (metal spatula); the underside should be lightly browned.

2 Carefully flip over the pancakes and cook for a further 30 seconds, or until the undersides are golden brown. Place the cooked pancakes in a dish lined with a clean dish towel and fold over the towel to keep them warm, while you cook the remaining mixture.

Below: Drizzle thin lines of crêpe batter into a hot pan to make lace crêpes.

Bottom: Use a spatula to flip over small pancakes made with thick batter.

TOPPING, FILLING AND SERVING

Below: You can top small pancakes with all kinds of ingredients – try a dollop of crème fraîche topped with a spoonful of caviar or a bitesize piece of smoked salmon.

Pancakes and crêpes are delicious served piping hot with a simple topping or filling, but they can also make the perfect base for a sophisticated snack, meal or dessert with very little time or effort involved. Many of the best fillings and toppings require little or no preparation or cooking.

TOPPING PANCAKES

Serving small, thick pancakes with a simple topping is probably the easiest way to turn a basic dish into an indulgent, sophisticated snack. Simply pile the toppings on to the pancakes and serve immediately. Alternatively, offer the pancakes with several bowls of different toppings and let your guests create their own combinations. Plain pancakes can be topped with either sweet or savoury ingredients, but batters flavoured with savoury ingredients such as herbs are best suited to savoury toppings, and pancakes made with a sweetened batter are best suited to sweet toppings.

SIMPLE SAVOURY TOPPINGS

The fabulous thing about pancakes is that many of the best toppings are incredibly simple and need virtually no preparation. Ready-made dips such as hummus and taramasalata make a perfect fuss-free choice. Try some of the following combinations spooned on to small plain or savoury pancakes. They taste delicious and look stunning served as a snack or appetizer.

- Spoon crème fraîche on to warm pancakes and top with strips of smoked salmon and a sprig of fresh dill.
- Spread each pancake thinly with a little chilli jam, then top with a sliver of goat's cheese and a couple of rocket (arugula) leaves.
- Spoon a little hummus on to each pancake and top with a strip of roasted red (bell) pepper and sprinkle over toasted pine nuts.
- Fold a strip of parma ham on to each pancake, then top with a dollop of ricotta cheese and a small wedge of ripe fig.
- Flavour good quality mayonnaise with pesto to taste, then spread thickly on pancakes and top with halved cherry tomatoes and fresh basil leaves.
- Spoon a little fresh tomato salsa on to each pancake, top with a small slice of avocado and garnish with a sprig of coriander (cilantro).

SWEET TOPPINGS

Small and bitesize pancakes served with sweet toppings make the ultimate treat for a special breakfast or tea. They're also great served for dessert – and are always a big hit with children, who love adding the toppings themselves. Try some of the sweet and sticky combinations suggested below, and watch the pancakes disappear as soon as you put them on the table.

Above left: Golden honey is great for drizzling over crêpes and pancakes.

Above: Flavour whipped cream with stem ginger or make fresh raspberry coulis for spooning over crêpes and pancakes.

- Top warm pancakes with a knob (pat) of butter and drizzle with maple syrup.
- Spread warm pancakes with a generous smear of clotted cream (heavy cream) and top with a spoonful of good quality strawberry conserve.
- Flavour mascarpone cheese with lemon zest and icing (confectioners') sugar to taste, then spoon on to warm pancakes and top with fresh raspberries.
- Finely chop preserved stem ginger and stir into a bowl of whipped cream. Stir in a little of the stem ginger syrup to taste, then spoon the mixture on to pancakes and top with small chunks of pineapple.
- Top each pancake with one or two slices of fresh mango and drizzle with summer fruit coulis. (To make the coulis, put about 250g/9oz summer fruits in a food processor and purée. Press the purée through a sieve to remove any pips, then sweeten with icing/confectioners' sugar to taste.)
- Cover each pancake with chocolate spread and top with chopped pistachio nuts.
- Top each pancake with Greek (US strained plain) yogurt and sprinkle with fresh blueberries and drizzle with honey.

FILLING PANCAKES AND CRÊPES

Paper-thin crêpes and large flat pancakes make perfect wrappers and can be rolled or folded in all manner of ways to enclose fillings. Once filled, they can be served immediately, or baked or fried in butter or oil until crisp and golden brown.

- To make a pancake roll, lay the pancake flat on a plate and place a few spoonfuls of filling on one side, then roll the pancake up around the filling.
- To fold a crêpe around a filling, lay the crêpe flat on a plate, spoon the filling on to one half of the crêpe and fold the other half on top over the filling.
- To make a crêpe parcel, lay the crêpe flat on a plate and place one or two spoonfuls of filling in the centre. Fold one side of the crêpe over the filling, then fold over the facing side. Fold up the remaining two sides and carefully flip over the parcel so that the folded sides are sitting underneath.
- To make a cone for filling, lay the crêpe flat on a plate, then fold it in half, then fold in half again. Carefully open up the cone and, holding the crêpe carefully so that it keeps its shape, spoon in the filling, then lay the filled pancake on a plate.

SAVOURY FILLINGS

Filling crêpes can be a more complex matter than topping pancakes, simply because there are so many different ways of filling and folding the crêpes. The fillings can be as simple or as complex as you choose, and the crêpes can be served immediately, baked in the oven or fried until crisp and golden. Listed below are a few simple ideas for filling and serving.

- Halve cherry tomatoes and arrange in a roasting pan or baking dish. Sprinkle over slivers of garlic and drizzle with olive oil. Roast at 220°C/425°F/Gas 7 for about 25 minutes. Spoon the roasted tomatoes on to crêpes, top with a spoonful of ricotta cheese and sprinkle with black pepper. Roll or fold up and serve immediately.
- Sauté finely chopped shallots until translucent, then add baby spinach and toss until wilted. Stir in crumbled feta cheese and season with black pepper and nutmeg. Roll or fold crêpes around the filling and serve immediately, or sprinkle with grated Parmesan cheese and bake at 200°C/400°F/Gas 6 for 15 minutes, or until golden.
- Stir cooked, peeled prawns (shrimp) into spicy tomato sauce and warm through. Fill crêpes and serve immediately.

Below: Simple savoury fillings work wonderfully well when wrapped in plain crêpes – roast ripe tomatoes with garlic, or sauté chopped shallots and spinach until wilted.

- Fry thinly sliced mushrooms in butter until they release their juices, then add strips of chicken breast and cook for about 5 minutes, or until the chicken is cooked through. Stir in crème fraîche and a handful of chopped fresh chives or tarragon, then season to taste with lemon juice, salt and ground black pepper. Fill crêpes with the mixture and bake at 200°C/400°F/Gas 6 for about 15 minutes, or until golden.

SWEET FILLINGS

Crêpes filled with sweet fruity or creamy fillings make delicious desserts. Try filling freshly cooked crêpes with some of the combinations suggested below.

- For the simplest filling, squeeze lemon juice over freshly cooked crêpes, sprinkle over caster (superfine) sugar and serve immediately.
- Place a scoop of ice cream or sorbet on each crêpe and fold in half to cover. Sprinkle icing (confectioners') sugar over the top, then serve immediately.
- Fill crêpes with fruit compote made from fresh or dried fruit and serve with a spoonful of crème fraîche.
- Fry slices of apple in butter, then sprinkle with dark brown sugar and a little cinnamon. Continue cooking until the sugar starts to caramelize, then spoon the fruit on to warm pancakes and fold over. Serve with a spoonful of whipped cream or crème fraîche, or a scoop of vanilla ice cream.
- Put sliced strawberries in a bowl and splash over a fruit liqueur such as Kirsch. Leave the fruit to mascerate for 30 minutes, then spoon on to pancakes and serve.
- Place two or three spoonfuls of sliced banana in the centre of each pancake and sprinkle over milk or dark chocolate chips. Fold the crêpe over the filling to make a parcel and bake at 200°C/400°F/Gas 6 for about 15 minutes, or until crisp and golden. Serve drizzled with honey and double (heavy) cream.

Above: There are lots of simple sweet crêpe fillings – try a scoop of ice cream, apple wedges fried with butter and sugar, or sliced strawberries.

STACKS and SNACKS

There's nothing so tempting as a stack
of piping hot pancakes, piled high and
drizzled with syrup for breakfast – or a
platter of delicate, bitesize morsels,
spread with a mouthwatering topping and
offered as a snack with drinks. They're
utterly fabulous served as an appetizer or
light meal, and make a perfect late-night
snack after a night out. Whatever time of
day, pancakes are perfect.

These small, thick, buttery pancakes are perfect for breakfast, but are equally good as a midnight treat after an evening out. They're so good that they'll be gone in seconds, so make plenty.

AMERICAN PANCAKES with BACON and SYRUP

STEP 1

STEP 3

makes about 20

INGREDIENTS

175g/6oz/1½ cups plain (all-purpose) flour, sifted

pinch of salt

15ml/1 tbsp caster (superfine) sugar

2 large (US extra large) eggs

150ml/¼ pint/⅔ cup milk

5ml/1 tsp bicarbonate of soda (baking soda)

10ml/2 tsp cream of tartar

oil, for cooking

butter

maple syrup

crisply grilled (broiled) bacon, to serve

1 To make the batter, combine the flour, salt and sugar. In a separate bowl, beat the eggs and milk together, then stir into the flour, beating to a smooth, thick consistency. Add the bicarbonate of soda and cream of tartar, mix well, then cover and chill until ready to cook.

2 When you are ready to cook the pancakes, beat the batter again. Heat a little oil in a heavy frying pan or griddle. Drop dessertspoonfuls of the mixture into the pan, spaced well apart, and cook over a fairly high heat until bubbles appear on the surface of the pancakes and the undersides become golden brown.

3 Carefully turn the pancakes over with a palette knife (metal spatula) and cook briefly until golden brown underneath, then transfer them to a heated serving dish. Top each pancake with a little butter and drizzle with maple syrup. Serve with grilled bacon.

COOK'S TIP
Make little tiny bitesize pancakes in advance and freeze for parties or children's teas.

Blinis are the classic leavened Russian pancakes. Traditionally served with sour cream and caviar, they have a very distinctive flavour and a marvellously fluffy, light texture.

BLINIS

1 Mix the buckwheat flour, plain flour, pepper and salt together in a large bowl.

2 In a small bowl, cream the yeast with 60ml/4 tbsp of the milk, then mix in the remaining milk.

3 Add the egg yolk to the flour mixture and gradually whisk in the yeast mixture to form a smooth batter. Cover with clear film (plastic wrap) and leave to stand in a warm place for 1 hour.

4 Whisk the egg white until it forms soft peaks, and fold into the batter. Lightly oil a heavy frying pan and heat it.

5 Pour in about 45ml/3 tbsp of the batter to make a 10cm/4in round pancake. Cook until the surface begins to dry out, then turn the pancake over using a fish slice or spatula and cook for 1–2 minutes. Repeat with the remaining batter. Serve warm topped with a spoonful of sour cream and a little caviar, garnished with dill sprigs.

VARIATION
If you prefer blinis with a stronger flavour, use all buckwheat flour, rather than a mixture of buckwheat and plain flours.

Makes about 10
INGREDIENTS

50g/2oz/½ cup buckwheat flour

50g/2oz/½ cup unbleached plain (all-purpose) flour

2.5ml/½ tsp freshly ground black pepper

5ml/1 tsp salt

15g/½oz fresh yeast

200ml/7fl oz/scant 1 cup lukewarm milk

1 egg, separated

sour cream and caviar, to serve

fresh dill sprigs, to garnish

STEP 2

STEP 4

STEP 5

Latkes are the little Jewish pancakes eaten at Chanukkah. The ones here contain spring onions and cottage cheese, which give a delicious flavour and lovely, gooey result.

MATZO MEAL LATKES

1 In a bowl, mash the cottage cheese. Mix in the egg yolks, half the salt, the matzo meal, onion, sugar, yogurt or water, and pepper.

2 Whisk the egg whites with the remaining salt until stiff. Fold one-third of the whisked egg whites into the batter, then fold in the remaining egg whites.

3 Heat the oil in a heavy frying pan to a depth of about 1cm/½in, until a cube of bread added to the pan turns brown immediately. Drop tablespoonfuls of the batter into the pan; fry over a medium-high heat until the undersides are golden brown. Turn the latkes carefully and fry the other side.

4 When cooked, remove each latke in turn from the pan with a slotted spoon and drain on kitchen paper. Serve immediately or place the latkes on a baking sheet and keep them warm in the oven.

VARIATION
To make sweet latkes, omit the sliced onion and add 15–30ml/1–2 tbsp sugar, a few chopped nuts and some ground cinnamon. Serve with a generous spoonful of fruit jam or honey.

Makes about 20

INGREDIENTS

275g/10oz/1¼ cups cottage cheese

3 eggs, separated

5ml/1 tsp salt

250g/9oz/2¼ cups matzo meal

1 onion, coarsely grated, or 3–5 spring onions (scallions), thinly sliced

2.5ml/½ tsp sugar

30–45ml/2–3 tbsp natural (plain) yogurt or water

ground black pepper

vegetable oil, for shallow frying

STEP 1

STEP 2

STEP 4

Little crisp golden pancakes made with shredded potato, flavoured with spring onion, then topped with crème fraîche and strips of smoked salmon make the ultimate appetizer.

POTATO PANCAKES with SMOKED SALMON

Makes about 12

INGREDIENTS

500g/1¼lb floury (starchy) potatoes

2 spring onions (scallions), thinly sliced

1 large (US extra large) egg

30ml/2 tbsp plain (all-purpose) flour

sunflower oil, for frying

250g/9oz smoked salmon

150ml/¼ pint/⅔ cup crème fraîche

salt and ground black pepper

chopped fresh dill or chives and caviar or salmon roe, to garnish

1 Preheat the oven to 140°C/275°F/Gas 1. Peel and grate the potatoes and place with the spring onions in a sieve. Press down with the back of a spoon to squeeze out as much starch as possible. Transfer to a bowl and add the egg and flour. Season and mix well.

2 Pour the oil into a large, deep non-stick frying pan or wok to a depth of 2cm/¾in and heat until it reaches 180°C/350°F, or when a cube of bread added to the oil browns in 45–60 seconds.

3 Carefully place a tablespoon of the potato mixture in the oil, flattening it slightly with the back of a spoon to form a small pancake about 5cm/2in in diameter.

4 Make more pancakes in the same way, cooking in batches and frying for 1 minute, until golden on the underside. Flip over and cook for 1–2 minutes more.

5 Remove the pancakes from the pan with a skimmer or slotted spoon and drain on a wire rack lined with kitchen paper. Transfer to a baking sheet and keep warm in the oven while you cook the remaining mixture.

6 Cut the salmon into strips. Place the pancakes on a serving plate and top each one with a spoonful of crème fraîche and strips of smoked salmon. Serve garnished with fresh dill or chives and caviar or salmon roe.

These little herby vegetable and Parmesan pancakes look stunning stacked high and topped with refreshing, spicy salsa. The batter and salsa can be prepared in advance.

VEGETABLE PANCAKES with TOMATO SALSA

STEP 1

STEP 3

Makes 10 to 12
INGREDIENTS
225g/8oz spinach

1 small leek

a few sprigs of fresh coriander (cilantro) or parsley

3 large (US extra large) eggs

50g/2oz/½ cup plain (all-purpose) flour, sifted

oil, for frying

25g/1oz/⅓ cup freshly grated Parmesan cheese

salt, ground black pepper and grated nutmeg

For the tomato salsa
2 tomatoes, peeled and chopped

¼ fresh red chilli, finely chopped

2 pieces sun-dried tomato in oil, drained and chopped

1 small red onion, chopped

1 garlic clove, crushed

60ml/4 tbsp good olive oil

30ml/2 tbsp sherry

2.5ml/½ tsp soft light brown sugar

1 Using a sharp knife, shred or chop the spinach with the leek and coriander or parsley until fine but not puréed. Alternatively, chop them in a food processor but do not over-process. Beat in the eggs and seasoning to taste. Gradually blend in the flour and 30–45ml/ 2–3 tbsp water and set aside for 20 minutes.

2 To prepare the tomato salsa, mix together all the ingredients in a bowl, stir gently, then cover and leave for 2–3 hours for the flavours to mingle.

3 To cook the pancakes, drop small spoonfuls of the batter into a lightly oiled non-stick frying pan and fry until golden underneath. Turn and cook briefly on the other side. Drain on kitchen paper and keep warm while you cook the remaining mixture.

4 Sprinkle the pancakes with grated Parmesan cheese and serve hot with the spicy tomato salsa.

VARIATION
Use watercress, sorrel or (Swiss) chard or a mixture of sorrel and chard in place of the spinach.

The fresh-flavoured salsa spiked with a little red onion and chilli complements these melt-in-the-mouth herby spring onion and ricotta pancakes perfectly.

RICOTTA PANCAKES with AVOCADO SALSA

1 Make the salsa first. Peel, stone and dice the avocados. Place in a bowl with the red onion, lime rind and juice. Add chilli to taste. Peel, seed and chop the tomatoes. Add them to the mixture, with the mint and coriander. Season with salt, pepper, sugar and Thai fish sauce. Mix well and set aside for 30 minutes.

2 Beat the ricotta until smooth, then beat in the egg and flour, then the milk to make a smooth, thick batter. Slice the spring onions and beat them in with the coriander. Season well with pepper and a little salt.

3 Heat a little oil in a large non-stick frying pan over a medium heat. Add spoonfuls of the mixture to make pancakes about 7.5cm/3in across. Fry for 4–5 minutes on each side, until set and browned. The mixture makes 12 ricotta pancakes.

4 Taste the salsa and adjust the seasoning, adding more lime juice and/or sugar if needed. Serve the pancakes immediately, with the avocado salsa and a large dollop of crème fraîche.

Serves 4 to 6

INGREDIENTS

250g/9oz/generous 1 cup ricotta cheese

1 large (US extra large) egg

90ml/6 tbsp self-raising (self-rising) flour

90ml/6 tbsp milk

6 spring onions (scallions)

30ml/2 tbsp chopped fresh coriander (cilantro)

sunflower oil, for shallow frying

salt and ground black pepper

crème fraîche, to serve

For the salsa

2 ripe, but not soft, avocados

1 small red onion, diced

grated rind and juice of 1 lime

$^1/_2$–1 fresh green or red chilli, seeded and finely chopped

225g/8oz tomatoes

30–45ml/2–3 tbsp chopped mint and coriander (cilantro)

pinch of sugar

5–10ml/1–2 tsp Thai fish sauce

STEP 1

STEP 2

These Scandinavian-style pancakes make a great appetizer or light meal served with salad. Alternatively, make little pancakes and serve them as canapés with shots of iced vodka.

CHIVE PANCAKES with PICKLED HERRING

STEP 1

STEP 4

Serves 6

INGREDIENTS

275g/10oz potatoes

2 eggs, beaten

150ml/¼ pint/⅔ cup milk

40g/1½oz/⅓ cup plain
(all-purpose) flour

30ml/2 tbsp chopped fresh
chives

vegetable oil or butter,
for greasing

salt and ground black pepper

For the topping

2 small red or yellow onions,
thinly sliced into rings

60ml/4 tbsp sour cream or
crème fraîche

5ml/1 tsp wholegrain mustard

15ml/1 tbsp chopped fresh dill

6 pickled herring fillets

fresh dill sprigs and fresh
chives or chive flowers,
to garnish

1 Cut the potatoes into chunks and cook them in boiling salted water for about 15 minutes, or until tender, then drain and mash or sieve to form a smooth purée.

2 Meanwhile prepare the topping. Place the onions in a bowl and cover with boiling water. Set aside for 2–3 minutes, then drain and dry on kitchen paper.

3 Mix the onions with the sour cream or crème fraîche, mustard and chopped dill. Season to taste.

4 Using a sharp knife, cut the pickled herring fillets into 12–18 pieces. Set them aside.

5 Put the potato purée in a bowl and beat in the eggs, milk and flour to make a batter. Season to taste with salt and pepper and whisk in the chives.

6 Heat a lightly greased non-stick frying pan. Spoon in 30ml/2 tbsp batter to make a pancake measuring 7.5cm/3in across. Cook for 3–4 minutes, until the underside is set and golden brown. Turn over and cook the other side, until golden brown. Keep warm while you make 11 more in batches of three to four.

7 Place two pancakes on each plate and add the onion topping and pieces of herring. Garnish with herbs, season with black pepper and serve immediately.

stacks and snacks **31**

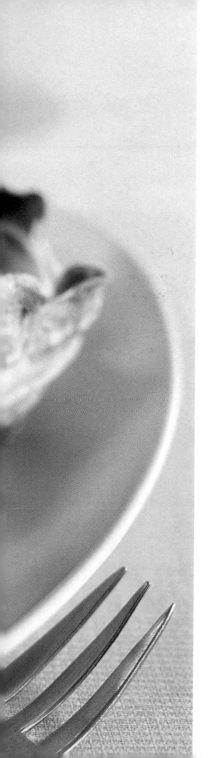

WRAPS and ROLLS

Crêpes and large flat pancakes are perfect for wrapping and rolling around fillings. They're unbelievably versatile and can be used to make all kinds of dishes. Depending on the choice of pancake and filling, pancake parcels and rolls can be served as a snack or light lunch, or as a more substantial meal or sophisticated dinner party dish. The variations are virtually endless, and always delicious.

These fabulous, golden lentil pancakes from southern India are served as a kind of bread, wrapped around spiced vegetables or curries. They are best eaten freshly cooked.

RED LENTIL DOSAS

Makes 6

INGREDIENTS

150g/5oz/³⁄₄ cup long grain rice

50g/2oz/¹⁄₄ cup red lentils

250ml/8fl oz/1 cup warm water

5ml/1 tsp salt

2.5ml/¹⁄₂ tsp ground turmeric

2.5ml/¹⁄₂ tsp freshly ground black pepper

30ml/2 tbsp chopped fresh coriander (cilantro)

oil, for frying and drizzling

1 Place the rice and lentils in a bowl, cover with the warm water and leave to soak for 8 hours.

2 Drain off the water and reserve. Place the rice and lentils in a food processor and blend until smooth.

3 Blend in the reserved water. Scrape into a bowl, cover with clear film (plastic wrap) and leave in a warm place to ferment for about 24 hours.

4 Stir in the salt, turmeric, pepper and coriander. Heat a heavy frying pan for a few minutes until hot. Smear with oil and add about 30–45ml/2–3 tbsp batter.

5 Using the rounded bottom of a soup spoon, gently spread the batter out, using a circular motion, to make a dosa 15cm/6in in diameter.

6 Cook for 1¹⁄₂–2 minutes, or until set. Drizzle a little oil over the dosa and around the edges. Turn over and cook for about 1 minute, or until golden. Keep warm while cooking the remaining dosas. Serve warm.

VARIATION
Add 60ml/4 tbsp grated coconut, 15ml/1 tbsp grated fresh root ginger and 1 finely chopped chilli to the batter just before cooking.

These bubbly, soft, buttery pancakes make perfect wraps. Roll them around spicy vegetable salads or garlicky roast tomatoes and sharp, creamy goat's cheese.

MIDDLE EASTERN YEASTED PANCAKES

1 In a bowl, dissolve the dried yeast and a pinch of the sugar in about 75ml/5 tbsp of the water. Leave in a warm place for about 10 minutes, or until frothy.

2 Add the remaining water and sugar, the flour, salt and melted butter or vegetable oil and mix to a smooth batter. Cover with a clean dishtowel, then leave in a warm place for about 1 hour, or until doubled in bulk.

3 Stir the thick, frothy batter and, if it seems too thick to ladle out, add a little extra water. Cover and leave in a warm place for about 1 hour.

4 Cook the pancakes in a non-stick frying pan. Spoon 45–60ml/3–4 tbsp of batter into the pan and cook over a low heat until the top is bubbling and the colour has changed. (Traditionally these pancakes are only cooked on one side, but they can be turned over and the second side cooked for just a moment if you wish.)

5 Remove the pancake from the pan and keep warm in a clean dishtowel while you cook the remaining batter.

COOK'S TIP
These pancakes are best eaten piping hot. Use two or three frying pans at the same time so that the pancakes are ready together.

Serves 4
INGREDIENTS

15ml/1 tbsp active dried yeast

15ml/1 tbsp sugar

500ml/17fl oz/2¼ cups lukewarm water

350g/12oz/3 cups plain (all-purpose) flour

5ml/1 tsp salt

50g/2oz/¼ cup butter, melted, or 60ml/4 tbsp vegetable oil

STEP 1

STEP 3

STEP 4

These wafer-thin crêpes filled with a mouthwatering soufflé mixture are baked to produce a crisp pancake pocket with a fabulous centre. They make a perfect vegetarian main course.

ARTICHOKE and LEEK CRÊPES

Serves 4

INGREDIENTS

115g/4oz/1 cup plain (all-purpose) flour

pinch of salt

1 egg

300ml/½ pint/1¼ cups milk

oil, for brushing

For the filling

60ml/4 tbsp butter

450g/1lb Jerusalem artichokes, peeled and diced

1 large leek, sliced thinly

30ml/2 tbsp self-raising (self-rising) flour

30ml/2 tbsp single (light) cream

75g/3oz mature (sharp) Cheddar cheese, grated

30ml/2 tbsp fresh parsley, chopped

fresh nutmeg, grated

2 eggs, separated

salt and ground black pepper

1 Put the flour, salt, egg and milk in a food processor and blend to make a smooth batter. Heat a 20cm/8in crêpe pan and lightly grease. Pour 30ml/2 tbsp of batter into the pan and swirl it around to coat. Cook for about 1 minute, or until golden underneath, then flip over and cook for 1 minute more.

2 Slide the pancake on to a plate and cover with a clean dishtowel while you cook another seven pancakes in the same way, stacking them under the towel.

3 To make the filling, melt the butter in a pan and add the artichokes and leeks. Cover and cook for 12 minutes until very soft. Mash with the back of a wooden spoon and season well.

4 Stir the flour into the vegetables and cook for about 1 minute. Remove from the heat and beat in the cream, cheese, parsley and nutmeg to taste. Leave to cool.

5 Preheat the oven to 190°C/375°F/Gas 5. Stir the egg yolks into the vegetable mixture. Whisk the whites until they form soft peaks and fold them into the mixture.

6 Grease a small ovenproof dish. Fold each pancake in four, hold the top open and carefully spoon the filling into the centre. Arrange the pancakes in the dish. Bake for 15 minutes until risen and golden. Serve at once.

Light, herby pancakes wrapped around a creamy spinach and pine nut filling, then baked make a delicious main meal. They are great served with a richly flavoured tomato sauce.

SPINACH-FILLED HERB CRÊPES

STEP 1

STEP 5

Serves 4

INGREDIENTS

25g/1oz/²/₃ cup chopped fresh herbs

15ml/1 tbsp sunflower oil, plus extra for frying

120ml/4fl oz/¹/₂ cup milk

3 eggs

25g/1oz/¹/₄ cup plain (all-purpose) flour

pinch of salt

For the filling

450g/1lb fresh spinach, cooked and drained

175g/6oz ricotta cheese

25g/1oz pine nuts, toasted

5 sun-dried tomato halves in olive oil, drained and chopped

30ml/2 tbsp shredded fresh basil

salt

grated nutmeg

ground black pepper

4 egg whites

oil, for greasing

1 To make the crêpes, place the herbs and oil in a food processor and blend until smooth. Add the milk, eggs, flour and salt and process again until smooth. Tip into a bowl, cover with clear film (plastic wrap) and leave to rest for 30 minutes.

2 Heat a small lightly greased non-stick frying pan and pour in a ladleful of the batter. Swirl the mixture to cover the base of the pan. Cook for 2 minutes, turn over and cook for a further 1–2 minutes. Make 7 more crêpes in the same way.

3 To make the filling, mix together the spinach with the ricotta, pine nuts, tomatoes and basil. Season with salt, nutmeg and pepper to taste.

4 Preheat the oven to 190ºC/375ºF/Gas 5. In a large, clean bowl, whisk the egg whites until stiff. Fold one-third of the egg whites into the spinach mixture, then gently fold in the rest.

5 Place one crêpe at a time on a lightly oiled baking sheet, add a spoonful of filling and fold into quarters. Bake for 12 minutes until set. Serve immediately.

These wonderful Chinese-style crab rolls are made with wafer-thin pancakes, which provide a very crisp case for the filling. They make a lovely appetizer or snack to serve with drinks.

CRISPY CRAB PANCAKE ROLLS

1 Make the pancake wrappers. Lightly beat the eggs and gradually stir in 450ml/¾ pint/scant 2 cups water. Sift the flour and salt into another bowl and gradually work in the egg mixture, and blend to a smooth batter. Leave to rest for 20 minutes, then whisk in an extra 15ml/1 tbsp cold water.

2 Lightly grease a 25cm/10in non-stick frying pan and heat gently. Pour in about 45ml/3 tbsp batter and swirl round the pan to spread evenly and very thinly. Cook for 2 minutes, or until loose underneath. There is no need to cook the pancake on the other side. Make more pancakes in the same way.

3 Combine the crab, spring onions, ginger, garlic, bamboo shoots, soy sauce, cornflour and egg yolk.

4 Lightly beat the egg white. Place a spoonful of filling in the middle of each pancake, brush the edges with egg white and fold into neat parcels, tucking in the ends.

5 Heat the oil in a deep-frying pan and fry 4 of the parcels, fold side downwards, for 1–2 minutes until golden and crisp. Remove and drain on kitchen paper. Keep warm in the oven while you cook the remaining egg rolls.

6 Garnish the rolls with spring onion curls and serve with the dipping sauce and wedges of lime.

Makes about 12

INGREDIENTS

3 eggs

175g/6oz/1½ cups plain (all-purpose) flour

2.5ml/½ tsp salt

oil, for deep frying

spring onion (scallion) curls, to garnish

45ml/3 tbsp light soy sauce mixed with 5ml/1 tsp sesame oil, for dipping

lime wedges, to serve

For the filling

225g/8oz/1⅓ cups crab meat

3 large spring onions (scallions), shredded

2.5cm/1in piece fresh root ginger, grated

2 large garlic cloves, chopped

115g/4oz bamboo shoots, chopped

15ml/1 tbsp soy sauce

10–15ml/2–3 tsp cornflour (cornstarch) blended with 15ml/1 tbsp water

1 egg, separated

STEP 1

STEP 2

These delicate herb-specked crêpes look delightful wrapped around the tangy chicken filling. Enjoy them as a simple mid-week supper or as a sophisticated dinner party dish.

CHICKEN with CHIVE PANCAKE PARCELS

Serves 4

INGREDIENTS

115g/4oz/1 cup plain (all-purpose) flour

1 egg, beaten

300ml/½ pint/1¼ cups milk

15ml/1 tbsp chopped chives

oil, for frying

For the filling

30ml/2 tbsp oil

450g/1lb/4 cups minced (ground) chicken

30ml/2 tbsp chopped chives

2 apples, cored and diced

25g/1oz/4 tbsp flour

175ml/6fl oz/¾ cup chicken stock

salt and black pepper

For the sauce

60ml/4 tbsp cranberry sauce

50ml/2fl oz/¼ cup chicken stock

15ml/1 tbsp clear honey

15g/½oz/2 tbsp cornflour (cornstarch)

1 Make the filling. Heat the oil in a large pan and fry the chicken for 5 minutes. Add the chives, apples and then the flour, then stir in the stock and seasoning. Cook over a gentle heat for 20 minutes.

2 To make the pancakes, sift the flour into a bowl together with a pinch of salt. Make a well in the centre and drop in the egg. Beat it in gradually with the milk to form a smooth batter.

3 Heat the oil in a 15cm/6in omelette pan, then pour off any excess and add one-quarter of the batter. Tilt the pan to coat the base and cook for 2–3 minutes. Turn the pancake over and cook for a further 2 minutes. Keep the pancakes warm, stacking them on top of each other, while you cook the remaining batter.

4 To make the sauce, put the cranberry sauce, stock and honey into a pan. Heat gently, stirring, until melted. Blend the cornflour with 20ml/4 tsp cold water, stir it in and bring to the boil. Cook, stirring until clear.

5 Lay the pancakes on a chopping board, spoon the filling into the centre of each one and fold over around the filling. Carefully lift the filled pancake on to a plate and spoon on the sauce. Serve immediately.

You need to begin this dish a couple of days ahead, but the result is worth it – delectable duck in wafer-thin pancakes spread with sauce and crisp cucumber and spring onions.

PEKING DUCK with MANDARIN PANCAKES

Serves 8

INGREDIENTS

1 duck, about 2.25kg/5lb

45ml/3 tbsp clear honey

5ml/1 tsp salt

30ml/2tbsp water

1 bunch spring onions (scallions), cut into strips

1 cucumber, seeded and cut into thin strips

120ml/4fl oz/$\frac{1}{2}$cup hoisin sauce and 120ml/4fl oz/$\frac{1}{2}$ cup plum sauce, for dipping

For the mandarin pancakes

275g/10oz/2$\frac{1}{2}$cups strong white bread flour, sifted

5ml/1 tsp salt

45ml/3 tbsp groundnut (peanut) oil

250ml/8fl oz/1 cup boiling water

1 Place the duck on a trivet in the sink and pour over boiling water. Drain, then tie the legs with string and hang the bird above a bowl in a cool place overnight. The next day, combine the honey, salt and water and brush half the mixture over the duck. Hang the bird up and leave for 3 hours. Repeat and leave for 3 hours.

2 Make the pancakes. Mix the flour and salt with one-third of the oil. Add the boiling water and mix to a soft dough. Knead for 3 minutes and rest for 30 minutes.

3 Preheat the oven to 230ºC/450ºF/Gas 8. Knead the dough and divide it into 24 pieces. Roll each to a 15cm/ 6in round. Brush half the rounds with oil and top each with a plain round. Cook each pancake pair in a lightly greased frying pan for 3 minutes, then turn over and cook for 3 minutes more. Separate the double pancakes and stack on a plate, with baking parchment between each one. Leave the pancakes to cool, then wrap in foil.

4 Put the duck on a rack in a roasting pan. Place it in the oven. Reduce the temperature to 180ºC/350ºF/Gas 4 and roast the duck for 1¾ hours without basting.

5 Reheat the parcel of pancakes in a steamer for 5–10 minutes. Carve the duck into small pieces. Spread the pancakes with dipping sauce, add duck, spring onions and cucumber and roll up. Serve immediately.

SWEET and SUMPTUOUS

Whether it's piping hot, spongy pancakes drenched in honey or delicate crêpes wrapped around a tantalizing filling – pancakes are the perfect base for a sweet treat. Crêpes filled with sorbet or creamy, fruity fillings, or flamed in an orange liqueur sauce make great desserts that are perfect after any meal.

These pancakes are smooth on one side, bubbly on the other and they melt in the mouth. Dripping with honey or drenched in sugar, they are often served for breakfast in Morocco.

MOROCCAN PANCAKES with HONEY

1 Place the yeast in a small bowl and add 30ml/2 tbsp lukewarm water. Break up the yeast with a spoon and gradually press and stir it into the water until dissolved. Add a little extra water, if necessary, so that the yeast forms a thin, creamy paste. Cover the bowl and leave in a warm place for about 15 minutes, until the surface is frothy and bubbly.

2 Sift the semolina and flour with the salt into a large bowl. Make a well in the centre and drop in the eggs. Heat the milk and water together until just warm, then pour into the well. Beat, gradually incorporating the flour, then add the yeast mixture and continue beating for 5 minutes to make a smooth batter. Cover the bowl with a cloth and leave the batter to rise in a warm place for at least 2 hours.

3 To cook the pancakes, heat a lightly oiled heavy pan. Pour in a small cupful of batter and spread evenly. Cook for about 2 minutes. Bubbles will form across the pancake and set in the batter. Lift out and wrap in a cloth to keep warm. Repeat with the remaining batter.

4 Spread the butter on the hot pancakes, or melt the butter in a wide pan and dip the pancakes into it. Serve warm with clear honey.

Makes 20 to 30
INGREDIENTS

40g/1½oz fresh yeast

400g/14oz/2¼ cups fine semolina

115g/4oz/1 cup plain (all-purpose) flour

5ml/1 tsp salt

3 eggs, lightly beaten

300ml/½ pint/1¼ cups milk

900ml/1½ pints/3¾ cups water

oil, for frying

75g/3oz/6 tbsp butter, at room temperature

clear honey, to serve

STEP 1

STEP 2

STEP 3

These delicious pancakes are made with a cider batter and filled with gloriously sticky, caramelized fried apples. Drizzled with honey and cream, they make the ultimate dessert.

APPLE-STUFFED CRÊPES

1 Make the batter. Sift the flour and salt into a large bowl. Add the eggs and milk and beat until smooth. Stir in the cider. Leave to stand for 30 minutes.

2 Heat a small heavy non-stick frying pan. Add a little butter and ladle in enough batter to coat the pan thinly.

3 Cook the crêpe for about 1 minute, until it is golden underneath, then flip it over and cook the other side until golden. Slide the crêpe on to a plate, then repeat with the remaining batter to make seven more. Set the crêpes aside and keep warm.

4 Make the apple filling. Core the apples and cut them into thick slices. Heat 15g/½oz butter in a large frying pan. Add the apples to the pan and cook until golden on both sides. Transfer the slices to a bowl with a slotted spoon and sprinkle with sugar.

5 Fold each pancake in half, then fold in half again to form a cone. Fill each with some of the fried apples. Place two filled pancakes on each dessert plate. Drizzle with a little honey and serve at once, with cream.

COOK'S TIP
For the best results, use full-fat (whole) milk to make the crêpe batter.

Serves 4
INGREDIENTS

115g/4oz/1 cup plain (all-purpose) flour

pinch of salt

2 large (US extra large) eggs

175ml/6fl oz/¾ cup milk

120ml/4fl oz/½ cup sweet cider

butter, for frying

120ml/8 tbsp clear honey, and 150ml/¼ pint/⅔ cup double (heavy) cream, to serve

For the filling

4 eating apples

60ml/4 tbsp caster (superfine) sugar

STEP 1

STEP 2

STEP 4

Baking these delicate citrus crêpes produces a lovely crisp case around the orange sorbet and mascarpone filling, which just begins to melt together to make a luscious dessert.

ORANGE CRÊPES with MASCARPONE CREAM

STEP 1

STEP 2

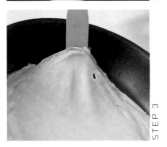

STEP 3

Serves 8

INGREDIENTS

115g/4oz/1 cup plain (all-purpose) flour

300ml/½ pint/1¼ cups milk

1 egg, plus 1 egg yolk

finely grated rind of 1 orange

30ml/2 tbsp caster (superfine) sugar

oil, for frying

For the filling

250g/9oz/generous 1 cup mascarpone cheese

15ml/1 tbsp icing (confectioners') sugar, plus extra, for dusting

90ml/6 tbsp single (light) cream

45ml/3 tbsp Cointreau or orange juice

500ml/17fl oz/2¼ cups orange sorbet (sherbet)

1 To make the crêpes, put the flour, milk, egg, egg yolk, orange rind and sugar in a food processor and blend until smooth. Pour the batter into a jug (pitcher) and leave to stand for 30 minutes.

2 Heat a little of the oil in a medium frying pan or crêpe pan until very hot. Drain off the excess. Pour a little of the batter into the pan, tilting the pan so that the batter coats the base thinly. Pour any excess back into the jug.

3 Cook the crêpe until the underside is golden, then flip it over with a palette knife (metal spatula) and cook the other side. Slide the crêpe on to a plate and cook seven more, lightly oiling the pan each time and stacking the cooked ones under a clean dishtowel.

4 Preheat the oven to 200°C/400°F/Gas 6. In a bowl, beat the mascarpone with the icing sugar, cream and Cointreau or orange juice until smooth. Spread the mixture on the crêpes, taking it almost to the edges.

5 Using a teaspoon, scoop shavings of sorbet and arrange them to one side of each topped crêpe. Fold the crêpes in half and dust with icing sugar. Fold again into quarters and dust with more icing sugar. Lay the crêpes in a large shallow baking dish and bake for 2 minutes, or until the sorbet starts to melt. Serve immediately.

Blintzes are a classic Jewish treat made from thin crêpe-like pancakes. The pancakes are cooked on one side, topped, then rolled to enclose the filling and pan-fried until golden brown.

ZESTY LEMON BLINTZES

1 To make the filling, put the cottage cheese in a sieve and leave for about 20 minutes to drain.

2 Put the cheese in a bowl and mash lightly with a fork. Add the beaten egg, lemon rind, sugar, sour cream and sultanas to the cheese and mix together.

3 To make the pancakes, whisk the eggs in a bowl, then add the water, salt and vegetable oil. Whisk in the flour and continue beating to form a smooth batter.

4 Heat a pancake pan, add a slick of oil, then ladle a little batter into the pan, swirling it to form a thin pancake. When it has set and the pancake edges have begun to lift, gently loosen the edges and flip the pancake on to a plate. Continue with the remaining batter to make about 8–12 pancakes, stacking them as you cook them. (They won't stick.)

5 Place 15–30ml/1–2 tbsp of the filling on the cooked side of a pancake and spread it out, leaving a border at the top and bottom. Fold in the top and bottom over the filling, then fold over one side and roll the pancake up carefully to enclose the filling completely.

6 To finish, heat the clean frying pan, add a little oil, then fry the rolled pancakes until golden brown underneath. Turn over and fry the second side. Serve hot.

Serves 4

INGREDIENTS

4 eggs

350ml/12fl oz/1½ cups water

pinch of salt

45ml/3 tbsp vegetable oil, plus extra, for frying

350g/12oz/3 cups plain (all-purpose) flour

For the filling

500g/1¼lb/2¼ cups cottage cheese

1 egg, lightly beaten

grated rind of ½–1 lemon

15–30ml/1–2 tbsp sugar

15–30ml/1–2 tbsp sour cream

30–45ml/2–3 tbsp sultanas (golden raisins)

STEP 3

STEP 4

STEP 5

These flaming crêpes drenched in a sweet, rich orange liqueur sauce are a classic French dessert. You can make the crêpes in advance, and put the dessert together at the last minute.

CRÊPES SUZETTE

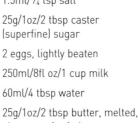

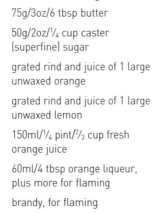

Serves 6

INGREDIENTS

115g/4oz/1 cup plain (all-purpose) flour

1.5ml/¼ tsp salt

25g/1oz/2 tbsp caster (superfine) sugar

2 eggs, lightly beaten

250ml/8fl oz/1 cup milk

60ml/4 tbsp water

25g/1oz/2 tbsp butter, melted, plus more for frying

For the orange sauce

75g/3oz/6 tbsp butter

50g/2oz/¼ cup caster (superfine) sugar

grated rind and juice of 1 large unwaxed orange

grated rind and juice of 1 large unwaxed lemon

150ml/¼ pint/⅔ cup fresh orange juice

60ml/4 tbsp orange liqueur, plus more for flaming

brandy, for flaming

orange segments, to serve

1 Sift the flour with the salt and sugar. Make a well in the centre and pour in the beaten eggs. Beat the eggs, gradually incorporating the surrounding flour, then whisk in the milk and water to make a smooth batter. Strain the batter into a large jug (pitcher) and set aside for 20–30 minutes.

2 Heat an 18cm/7in crêpe pan. Stir the melted butter into the batter. Grease the pan and pour in about 30ml/ 2 tbsp of batter. Quickly tilt the pan to cover the base. Cook for 1 minute until the top is set and the base is golden. Turn over and cook for 20–30 seconds. Slide on to a plate. Make more crêpes in the same way.

3 To make the sauce, melt the butter in a large frying pan, then stir in the sugar, orange and lemon rind and juice, the additional orange juice and the liqueur.

4 Place a crêpe in the pan, browned-side down, swirling to coat with the orange sauce. Fold it in half, then in half again to form a triangle and push to the side of the pan. Continue heating and folding the crêpes until all are warm and covered with the sauce.

5 Heat 30–45ml/2–3 tbsp each of orange liqueur and brandy in a small pan. Remove the pan from the heat, ignite the liquid, then carefully pour over the crêpes. Scatter over the orange segments and serve immediately.

Pretty lace pancakes filled with sorbet make a stunning dinner party dessert. The sweet yet tangy cranberry sorbet can be made using fresh or frozen cranberries.

CRANBERRY SORBET in LACE PANCAKES

1 Heat the cranberries, sugar and orange juice in a pan, stirring until the sugar has dissolved. Cook for 5–8 minutes, until the cranberries are very tender. Leave to cool, then purée in a food processor. Press the purée through a sieve placed over a bowl to extract all the juice. Stir in the liqueur and chill.

2 Pour the mixture into a shallow container and freeze for 3–4 hours, beating twice. Alternatively, make the sorbet in an ice-cream maker. Freeze until solid.

3 Make the pancakes. Sift the flour and ginger into a bowl. Add the egg, sugar and a little of the milk. Gradually whisk in the remaining milk to make a smooth batter.

4 Heat a little oil in a crêpe pan, pour off the excess and drizzle over a little of the batter to make a lacy pancake. Cook gently until golden underneath, then carefully turn over, and cook for 1 minute more. Slide on to a plate. Make five more pancakes in the same way, lightly oiling the pan each time.

5 To serve, lay a pancake on a serving plate, underside upwards. Arrange several small scoops of the sorbet on one side of the pancake, then fold the crêpe over the sorbet and dust generously with icing sugar. Scatter with extra cranberries and serve with whipped cream.

Serves 6

INGREDIENTS

50g/2oz/½ cup plain (all-purpose) flour

2.5ml/½ tsp ground ginger

1 egg

15ml/1 tbsp caster (superfine) sugar

120ml/4fl oz/½ cup milk

a little oil, for frying

For the filling

500g/1¼lb/4 cups cranberries

225g/8oz/1 cup caster (superfine) sugar

300ml/½ pint/1¼ cups orange juice

60ml/4 tbsp Cointreau or other orange liqueur

icing (confectioners') sugar, for dusting

extra cranberries and lightly whipped cream, to serve

STEP 3

STEP 4

These coffee-flavoured crêpes are made with buckwheat flour and have a wonderfully light texture. The sweet, juicy, golden peaches and cream complement them perfectly.

COFFEE CRÊPES with PEACHES and CREAM

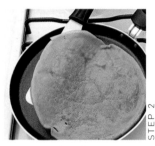

STEP 2

STEP 3

Serves 6

INGREDIENTS

75g/3oz/²⁄₃ cup plain (all-purpose) flour

25g/1oz/¹⁄₄ cup buckwheat flour

1.5ml/¹⁄₄ tsp salt

1 egg, beaten

200ml/7fl oz/scant 1 cup milk

15g/¹⁄₂oz/1 tbsp butter, melted

100ml/3¹⁄₂fl oz/scant ¹⁄₂ cup strong brewed coffee

sunflower oil, for frying

For the filling

6 ripe peaches

300ml/¹⁄₂ pint/1¹⁄₄ cups double (heavy) cream

15ml/1 tbsp Amaretto liqueur

225g/8oz/1 cup mascarpone cheese

65g/2¹⁄₂oz/generous ¹⁄₄ cup caster (superfine) sugar

30ml/2 tbsp icing (confectioners') sugar, for dusting

1 Sift the flours and salt into a mixing bowl. Make a well in the centre and add the egg, half the milk and the melted butter. Gradually mix in all the surrounding flour, beating until smooth, then beat in the remaining milk and coffee.

2 Heat a drizzle of oil in a 15–20cm/6–8in crêpe pan. Pour in just enough batter to thinly cover the base of the pan. Cook for 2–3 minutes, until the underside is golden brown, then flip over and cook the other side.

3 Slide the crêpe out of the pan on to a plate. Make more crêpes in the same way, stacking the cooked crêpes and interleaving them with baking parchment.

4 To make the filling, halve the peaches and remove the stones. Cut into thick slices. Whip the cream and Amaretto liqueur until soft peaks form, then beat the mascarpone and sugar until smooth. Beat 30ml/2 tbsp of the whipped cream into the mascarpone, then fold in the remainder.

5 Spoon a little of the Amaretto cream on to one half of each crêpe and top with peach slices. Gently fold the pancake over. Dust with icing sugar and serve.

INDEX

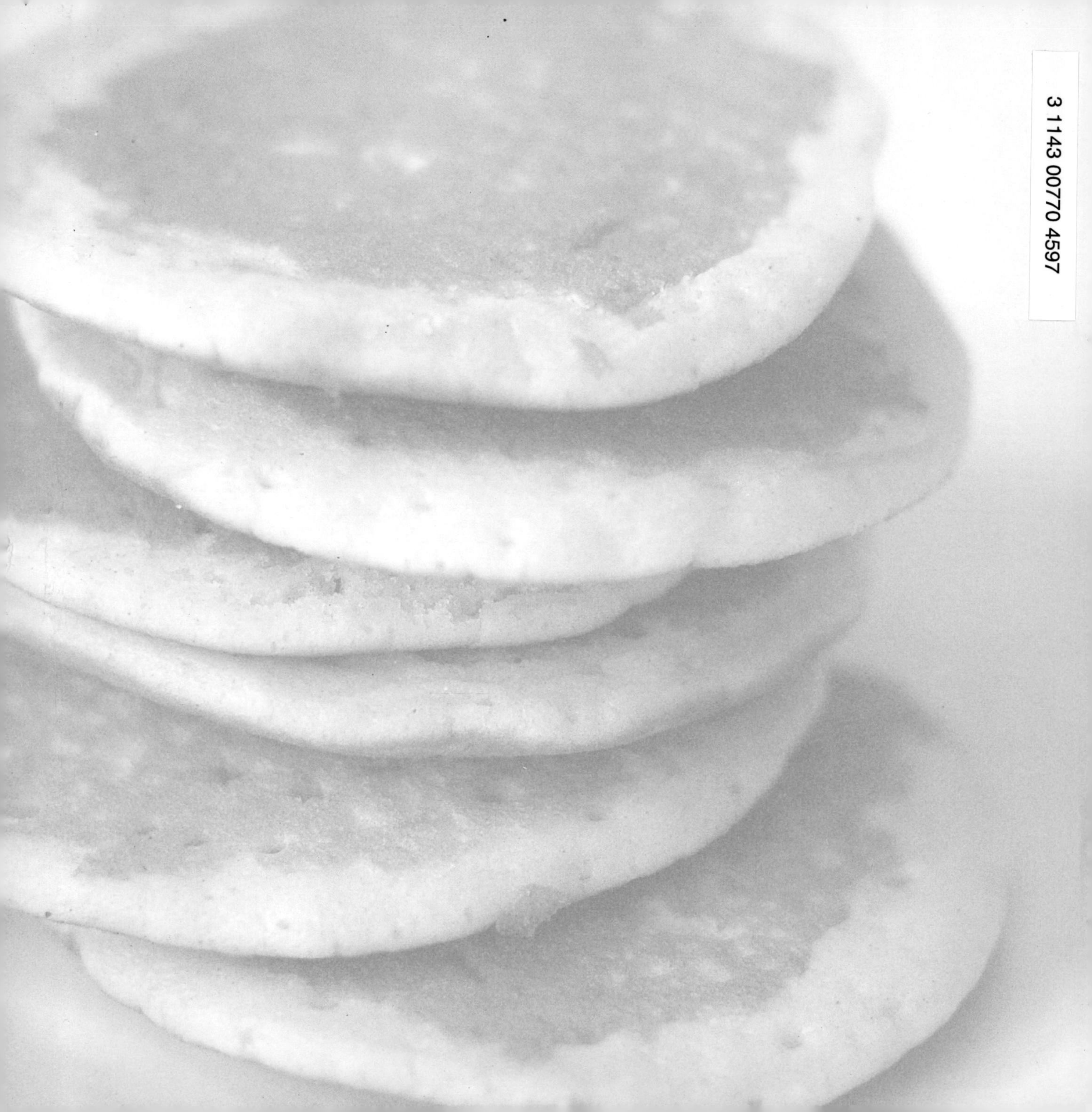